History in Evidence

LIFE IN IRON AGE BRITAIN

MARGARET HERDMAN

13. 3. 81.

Harrap

First published in Great Britain 1981

by GEORGE G. HARRAP & CO. LTD
182 High Holborn, London WC1V 7AX

© *Margaret Herdman* 1981

ISBN 0 245 53534 9

Phototypeset in V.I.P. Sabon
by Western Printing Services Ltd, Bristol
Printed in Great Britain
by J. W. Arrowsmith Ltd, Bristol

Timeline for Prehistoric Britain

Old Stone Age/Palaeolithic
During the Ice Age man the toolmaker first appeared in Britain. Mammoths, woolly rhinoceros and reindeer were hunted over the plains for food and were skinned and cut up with flint hand axes.   c 10 000 BC

Middle Stone Age/Mesolithic
As the climate grew warmer after the Ice Age, forests covered the land. People gathered their food, fished and hunted using flint tipped arrows and bone spearheads.   c 3500 BC

New Stone Age/Neolithic
The first farmers came across the sea from the Continent bringing seed corn and domestic animals. Polished flint axes were used to clear the trees for crop-growing. Pottery was made for the first time, the dead were buried in communal graves marked by long barrows and large monuments called henges were built.   c 2000 BC

Bronze Age
The first metal users appeared in Britain. Copper then bronze slowly began to replace flint for axes, knives then swords. Individuals were buried in round barrows. Stonehenge reached its final form.   c 700 BC

Iron Age
Iron working began in south-east Britain. The use of iron for tools and weapons spread northwards but it remained a precious metal until late in the Iron Age. People lived in small farms and constructed forts on hill tops, mainly in the south and east.   AD 43

Roman Period
The Roman Emperor Claudius conquered south-east Britain in AD 43. Roman power spread westwards and northwards through Britain. The frontier at Hadrian's Wall was built around AD 127. The Roman troops were finally withdrawn at the beginning of the fifth century AD. The last appeal to Rome by the Britons for military aid against invaders was recorded in . . .   AD 446

Maiden Castle near Dorchester in Dorset is one of the largest British hillforts. Its many ramparts and ditches developed over hundreds of years and enabled the occupants to defend themselves against their enemies with slings and spears

In AD 43 the Roman general Vespasian captured the fort and slaughtered some of its inhabitants whose bodies were buried near one of the gateways

Britain in the Iron Age

Hillforts

If you have walked on the chalk hills of Sussex, Hampshire and Dorset or along the limestone ridge of the Cotswolds you may have stumbled across earthworks, banks and ditches enclosing the hill top. Look at an Ordnance Survey map of any high ground in southern England and you will notice that ancient forts or camps are frequently marked. They are less common in other parts of Britain.

These enclosures, which are roughly circular in plan, are hillforts made by people more than 2000 years ago. There are about 3000 hillforts mostly in the south and east of the country varying greatly in size and shape. Usually the forts are on hill tops, or on headlands projecting into the sea, but a few are found on lower ground.

One of the most impressive and best known of British hillforts is Maiden Castle in Dorset. From the picture you will see that it covers a vast area, is surrounded by several steep banks and ditches and has two complicated entrances. But not all hillforts are as massive as Maiden Castle and their defences may not be so formidable. These variations in scale probably reflect different histories and different uses.

People

The people who built the hillforts lived in the period called the Iron Age, which lasted for roughly 800 years until the Roman invasion of southern Britain under the Emperor Claudius in AD 43. The Iron Age is the final phase of the prehistoric period. History begins from the time when written records began to be kept, and writing was not brought to Britain until the time of the Romans. Because the Iron Age people and the people before them left no written records to tell us about themselves we call this period *pre-history*.

By just looking at hillforts we can begin to think about life in the Iron Age. The size of the forts suggests that it must have taken a large number of people a long time to build one of them in an age without machines. A massive project like building a hillfort can only have been undertaken by a well-organized society working under the direction of a chieftain. But you may ask — how did they build the forts and, perhaps even more important, why? We have to search for other ways to find out.

Written Evidence

The Roman writers who came into contact with the later Iron Age people in Britain give us some information about them and their country. For example Julius Caesar, writing at the time of his expedition in 55 and 54 BC, says that the population was large and lived mostly in scattered farms, although he does mention fortifications as well. This kind of information is useful, but we need a lot more evidence to answer some of the questions that arise about these people. It is the archaeological remains, not just hillforts but other things which have survived, that tell us about their daily life.

Pottery and Dating

The archaeologist usually finds broken pieces of pottery called sherds. These are cleaned by washing or dry brushing and are clearly marked to show exactly where and at what depth on the site they have been found. Sometimes several sherds of one pot are recovered and may be stuck together to reconstruct at least part of the pot. This gives a better idea of its shape and size. Much of the pottery is then drawn so that the shapes and sizes as well as the kinds of clay, colour and decoration are recorded.

Just as fashions and styles change today so styles and designs of pots are related to their age. The archaeologist, by studying the different types of pot, may be able to arrange them in order of age. This is tested by comparing the pots found in the stratified layers of the archaeological site — the sherds of pot found in the bottoms of pits and the lower layers are older than those in the layers above. (See p. 37 for further explanation.)

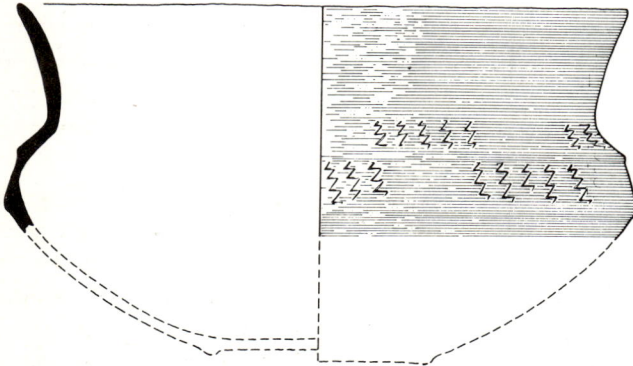

An archaeological drawing of a 5th Century BC pot. This method of drawing records the shape, the thickness and the decoration of the pot

Notice the difference in shape and decoration of this 2nd Century BC pot. Pieces or sherds of pottery like those in the foreground are found on excavations. Occasionally several sherds of one pot are recovered and may be pieced together with the missing bits made up with plaster of Paris or a resin substance

Try producing your own *typology* or order of age for any group of objects such as cars, shoes, postcards or even hairstyles.

Archaeological Finds

What sort of remains does the archaeologist look for? What things does he find that have survived for more than 2000 years? Look around the room you are now in and see if you can suggest what things might still exist in 2000 years from today.

Baked clay pots are some of the most long-lasting man-made objects used by prehistoric people. In fact although pottery may be broken it is practically ever-lasting unless ground into dust. The different clay used to make pots and their shape, style and decoration provide clues about the cooking and eating habits and the skills of the people who made and used them. A study of the changing types of pot tells the expert roughly when a pot was made, just as you may be able to guess the age of a car by its design. In this way a pot or sherds (fragments) of pottery found in the scrabblings of a rabbit burrow at the base of a rampart indicate the century when the hillfort was in use.

Bones also survive in some soils and these may tell us the kinds of animals kept and hunted. From human bones we learn the size of the people, how long they lived and sometimes what illnesses and diseases they suffered from.

Various metals are sometimes preserved; our museums contain iron tools and weapons used in everyday life, also bronze and sometimes gold jewellery dating from the Iron Age.

Excavation

Although these individual things can tell us quite a lot, their use becomes much clearer if we know where Iron Age people dropped or placed them. Archaeologists who study prehistory first use all the information they can get by looking at the earthworks and by examining objects. Then, to discover more about the daily life of the people, where they lived, or why the hillforts were built, they look beneath the surface of the ground, in other words they have to excavate.

Some of the remains, such as those of the Iron Age houses, are so slight that they may easily be destroyed if the archaeologist does not dig with extreme care, and record exactly what he finds. Gradually, however, our knowledge of Iron Age life and how it was organized is increasing, and although the picture can never be complete, since much evidence has already disappeared, there is still a lot to be discovered about life in Britain from around 700 BC until AD 43.

Archaeological excavation at Danebury hillfort, Hampshire

The People

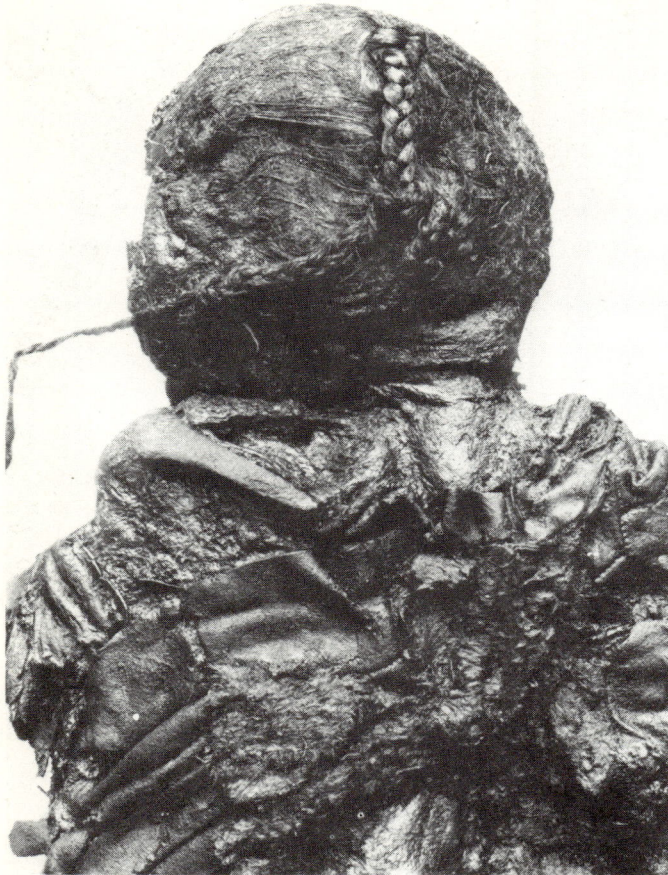

Very occasionally discoveries are made which allow us to picture Iron Age people. This body preserved in a peat bog at Tollund Fen in Denmark is one of the few pieces of archaeological evidence we have of Iron Age hairstyles

The people of the Iron Age both in Britain and on the Continent looked and dressed very differently from the Romans who conquered them. Most of our information about their looks and clothes comes from the classical writers, mainly Romans, who were struck by these differences.

Many of these writers mention the fair skins of the Iron Age people of Britain and their neighbours in Gaul, which must have contrasted strikingly with the dark hair and olive skins of Mediterranean peoples. The Greek writer, Strabo, says that their hair was naturally fair, but that they also used artificial means to lighten it. He says they washed their hair with lime wash and brushed it back from the forehead so that it stood up like a horse's mane. Both men and women wore their hair long, and it often seems to have been plaited

This bucket ornament from Welwyn in Hertfordshire shows an Iron Age man's head with brushed-back hair

8

Iron Age man sometimes produced pictures of himself like this coin from south-east England. Compare the hairstyle with what Strabo tells us

Also of interest to the Romans were the beards and moustaches of the Britons. Diodorus Siculus, a historian, says that some of the men wore short beards, while others shaved their chins but let their moustaches grow long. 'And so when they are eating the moustache becomes entangled in the food, and when they are drinking the drink passes, as it were, through a sort of strainer.'

These people seem to have been very concerned with their personal appearance. According to Strabo, the men of this period in barbarian Europe were weight conscious and considered it disgraceful to become fat. Not only were the men tall and strong, but the women are mentioned as being equally well-built.

The more wealthy Iron Age people were sometimes buried with their favourite possessions. The grave of a woman found at Birdlip Hill, Gloucestershire, includes these objects — her mirror, beads, rings and a brooch

Their use of cosmetics is recorded by Roman writers, and archaeologists have found many fine mirrors and razors used perhaps by the wealthier people, as well as beautiful jewellery for personal adornment.

Roman writers describing the Iron Age peoples of Europe often mentioned their strange habit of wearing trousers. This section from the Gundestrup cauldron found buried in a bog in Denmark gives us some idea of what Iron Age trousers perhaps looked like. We have no similar evidence from Britain, but it is probable that the Britons dressed like their continental neighbours

Clothes

The main difference between the clothes of the Iron Age people and the Romans is that the Britons and Gauls wore bright colours and some of the men wore close-fitting trousers. Diodorus Siculus says the people of Gaul wore tunics which were dyed and stained various colours, trousers, and over these striped woollen cloaks, fastened with buckles. In summer they wore light cloaks with a checked pattern.

Dio Cassius, a Roman historian writing in the third century AD, gives us some idea of women's dress with his description of the British Queen Boudica: 'A great mass of bright red hair fell to her knees ... She wore a great twisted golden necklace and a tunic of many colours, over which was a thick mantle, fastened by a brooch.'

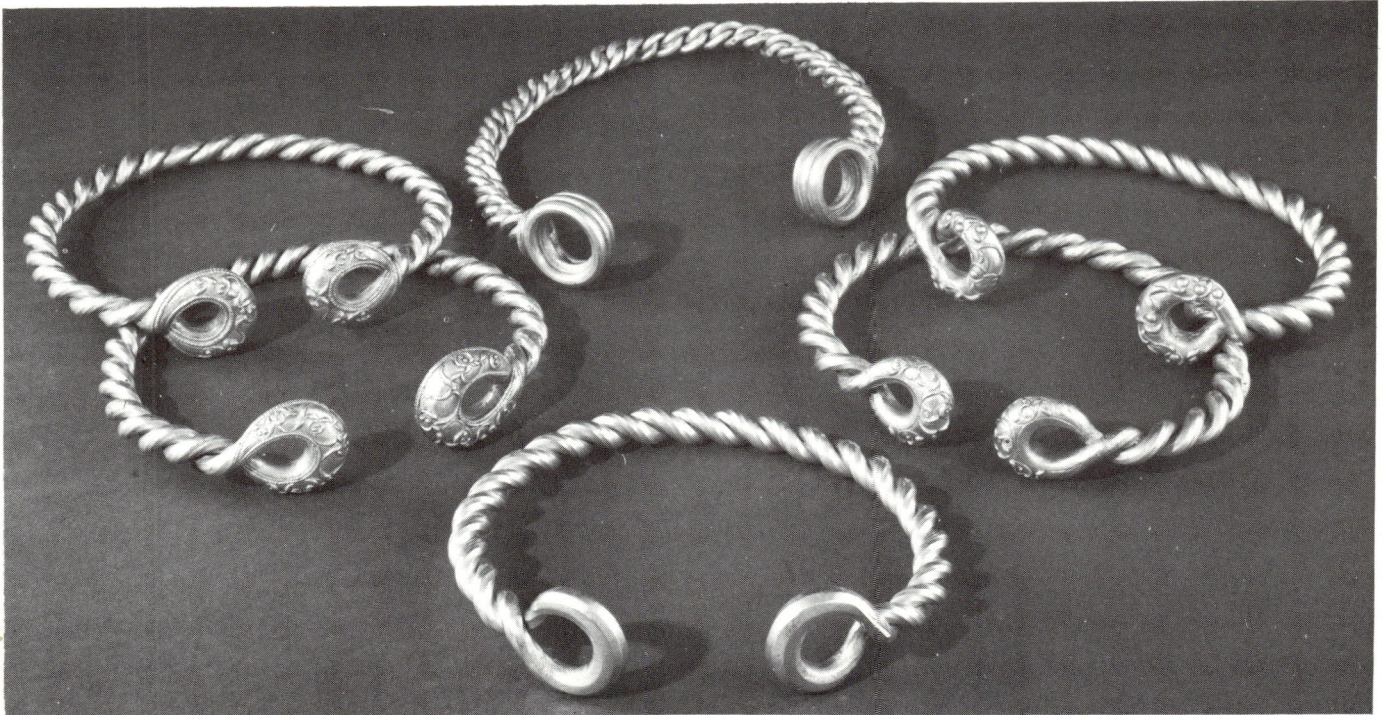

The six great gold torques were dug up at Ipswich. They would have been of enormous value — perhaps they belonged to a wealthy chieftain, but they may have been offerings to the gods

Neck torques, we are told by classical writers, were thought by the Iron Age peoples of Europe to give magical protection. The man on the Gundestrup cauldron is wearing such a torque

Woollen cloaks from Britain and Gaul were exported throughout the Roman empire, and the Birrus Britannica (a type of woollen cloak from Britain) was heavily taxed.

Together the scraps of written evidence and the archaeological finds help to give us some idea of how the Iron Age people looked. However, Julius Caesar tells us that when he invaded Britain in 55 and 54 BC, the tribes living in the interior were wearing skins. He goes on to say that they dyed their bodies blue with a plant called woad, wore their hair long and shaved all their bodies except the head and the upper lip. This description is probably an over-simplification, and perhaps he meant that some of the cattle farmers in the north wore clothes made from skins and the blue dye may refer to war paint used by the warriors going into battle against the Roman army.

Behaviour

Towards the end of the Iron Age in Britain, the people had developed a decidedly warlike attitude and several Roman writers comment on this. There were two features of their warfare which struck the Romans as unusual. One was the way they used chariots in battle, and the other was the custom of single combat. Caesar talks at length about the Britons using chariots when fighting against his army. He says

> In chariot fighting the Britons begin by driving all over the field hurling javelins, and generally the terror inspired by the horses and the noise of the wheels are enough to throw their opponents' ranks into disorder.

He goes on to say that the warriors then jump down from their chariots and engage in single combat, while the charioteers retire and wait at a short distance, ready to collect the warriors should this be necessary. In this way they combined the mobility of cavalry with the staying power of infantry. Caesar also talks about

Britain was well known for the quality of its woollen cloaks throughout the Roman period and sometimes Roman carvings show natives wearing them. (This one is from Cirencester in Gloucestershire.) Cloaks of this sort had probably changed little since the Iron Age

12

the skill with which the chariots were driven and how the charioteers could run along the chariot pole, stand on the yoke and get back into the chariot as quick as lightning.

Using the description of the British war chariot which Julius Caesar gives us, and adding to it the archaeological evidence from the metal fittings of such a chariot, it has been possible for archaeologists to make this model. Perhaps you could design an alternative model based on the same evidence. Unless we find an actual chariot preserved, we are unlikely ever to be able to make a more accurate reconstruction

The many weapons which have been found further emphasize the warlike nature of the Britons. Iron daggers, swords and spears were used by the warriors, and a large number of these weapons have been recovered from the rivers where they were possibly thrown as offerings to the gods. Shields are less often found, as they were normally made of wood and leather, but towards the end of the period a few elaborate bronze shields were made.

This magnificent bronze shield was dredged from the River Thames at Battersea

13

Like the shield (p. 13) this helmet was found in the Thames near Waterloo Bridge. They were both probably items of display and may even have been made deliberately to be sacrificed to the gods — we shall never know, but the fact that they were thrown into the river would suggest that they were offered to the gods

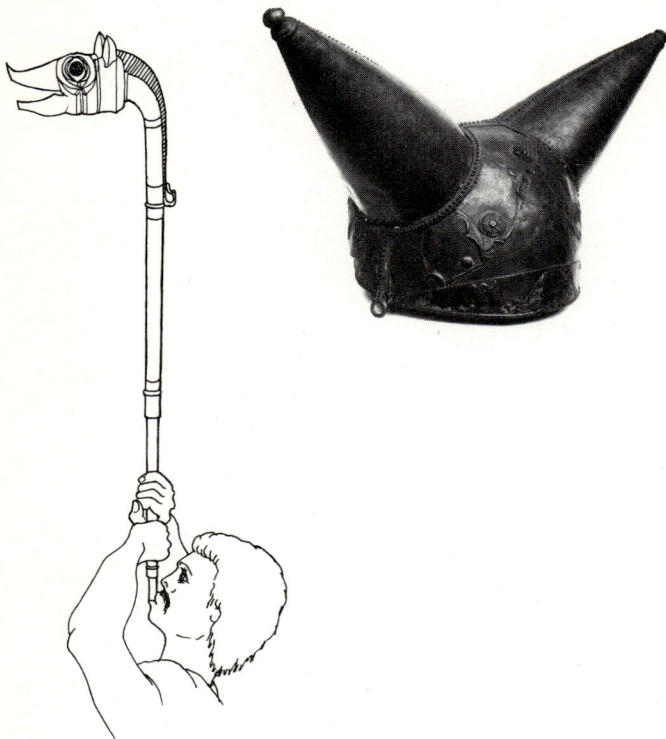

The carnyx was a tall war trumpet with its end shaped like an animal's head. It was blown by Iron Age warriors in battle probably to frighten the enemy with its noise.

Such carnyxes are illustrated on the Gundestrup cauldron and the remains of an actual instrument have been found in Lincolnshire

Diodorus Siculus describes how the Britons appeared in battle:

Their armour includes man-sized shields decorated in individual fashion. . . . On their heads they wear bronze helmets. . . . Some have iron breast plates of chain mail while others fight naked. . . . Instead of the short sword they carry long swords. . . . The spears they brandish in battle have iron heads a cubit or more in length.

By the end of the Iron Age in Britain, then, much wealth and skill went towards equipping heroes with fine weapons and shields, showing just how important war and fighting had become, at least to the aristocratic classes.

Other scraps of information can be gleaned from the classical writers. Julius Caesar, in the first century BC, mentions a large population of cattle farmers. Another writer, Suetonius, talks about hillforts when describing the campaigns of the Roman general Vespasian during the conquest of Britain in the middle of the first century AD. We learn the names of tribes in Britain at the time of the conquest, for at this stage the country was divided into territories and ruled by tribal chieftains. For the first time we hear of individual chieftains by name. Caesar, for instance, mentions one such, Commius, whose kingdom in Britain stretched from Sussex to Berkshire.

To find out about the daily life of the average Iron Age family, however, we must leave the writers and turn to the evidence provided by excavation.

The Farms

Caesar said Britain was a land of small farms and archaeology has proved him correct. More and more Iron Age farm sites are being discovered over the whole country from the Shetland Islands to Cornwall. They date from as early as 1000 BC until well into the Roman period. Each farm must have supported a family group — including mother and father, three, four or more children, grandfather and grandmother, uncles and aunts. All of them worked on the land to produce enough food to live on and a little extra to exchange for things they could not grow or make.

Here are some examples of Iron Age Farms that have been discovered in different parts of Britain.

Farley Mount, Hampshire

Opposite, an Iron Age farm shows up on the aerial photograph. It has not been excavated but you can see a circular ditch and bank enclosing the farmstead, with acres of rectangular fields bounded by banks spreading out from the farm. The fields are small and were used for crop growing, although the Iron Age farmer would have kept animals as well to provide the manure to fertilize his fields. Alternate fields would have been left fallow each year to rest the soil. Cattle have to be fed and sheltered in winter, so they would have been kept close to the living quarters of the family. The big enclosure at Farley Mount was probably for the animals, so the houses for the family are likely to have been in that corner of the enclosure which is separated by another ditch.

Aerial photograph of the Iron Age farm at Farley Mount

Mingies Ditch — Hardwick, Oxfordshire

This farmstead is in the Thames valley on the river gravels which were laid down during the Ice Ages more than 80 000 years ago. People have lived on the gravels since Palaeolithic times and there were many farms here in the Iron Age. The farmstead at Hardwick was discovered because two dark rings were noticed on photographs taken from an aeroplane.

Although if you walked across this field you would have no reason to guess that you were on the site of an Iron Age farm, from the air the plan of the farm can be picked out. Look at the archaeologist's plan of the site after it had been excavated and see if you can match it with the photograph.

The dark marks on the photographs are caused by the rich green of the crop growing over the deeper and damper soil which fills the Iron Age ditches. The rest of the crop has begun to ripen and is a paler colour

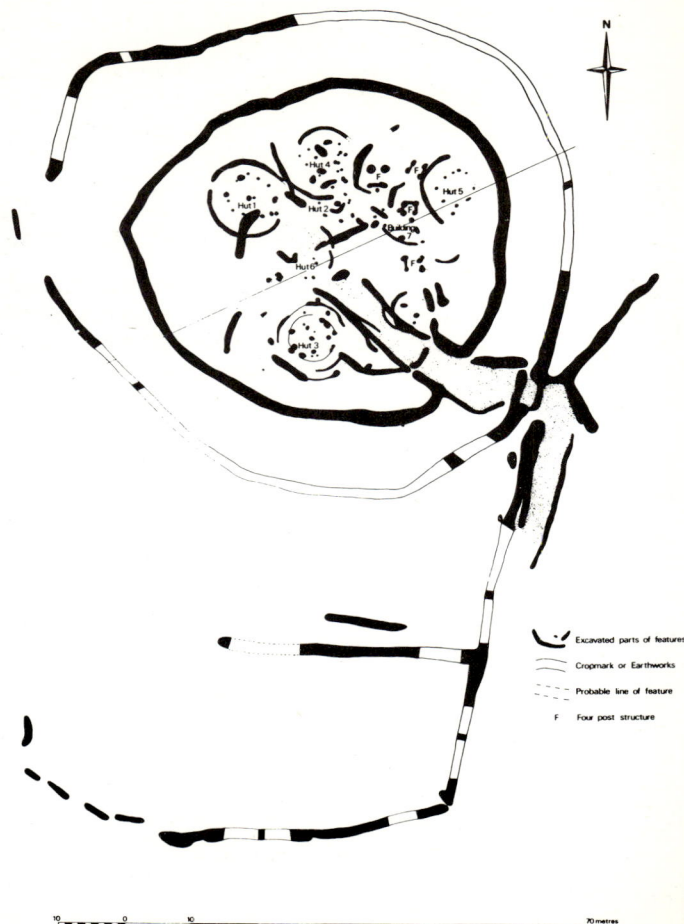

HARDWICK with YELFORD
MINGIES DITCH 1977-8

Excavated parts of features
Cropmark or Earthworks
Probable line of feature
F   Four post structure

16

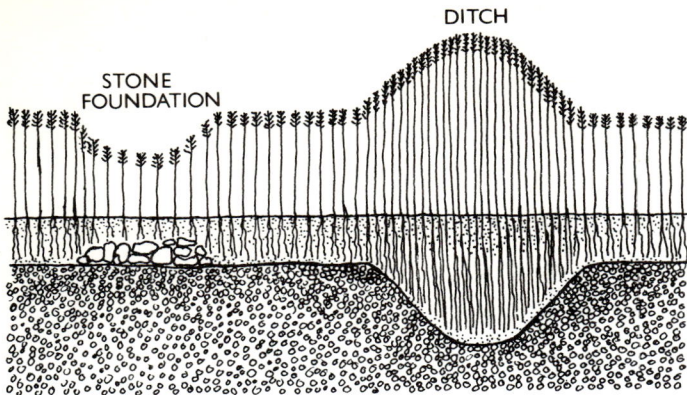

Cropmarks are caused by grain growing taller over buried pits or ditches, which were cut into the subsoil and have become silted up with richer topsoil. Buried stone foundations cause the crop to grow less tall and in very dry weather brownish parch marks may appear

It was decided to excavate the two rings before gravel quarrying in the area could destroy any remains. When the archaeologists removed the topsoil they found that the rings marked two ditches enclosing the farm. They were about a metre deep, and, on top of the low bank formed beside each one when it was dug, a thick hedge would have been planted. These hedges and ditches were probably meant to keep out wild animals and to keep in the farm animals rather than as a defence against unfriendly neighbours. There were remains of houses within the area enclosed by the inner ditch, but nothing was found between the inner and outer ditches, so this part was probably used to protect and shelter the animals. There was a gap in the outer ditch on the side near the stream so the animals could have reached water easily.

Traces of at least six round houses all about six metres in diameter were found but they could not all have been standing and in use at the same time. Can you see from the archaeologist's plan why this is so? Houses were pulled down and replaced when they became old and leaky. The holes for the door posts of these houses survived and a burnt patch of earth and stones in the middle of the floor showed where the fireplace was. The walls of one house were marked by the stakeholes between which smaller twigs or *wattles* would have been woven. The timber work was then plastered with *daub* — a mixture of mud, straw, animal hair and dung — to make the walls weatherproof.

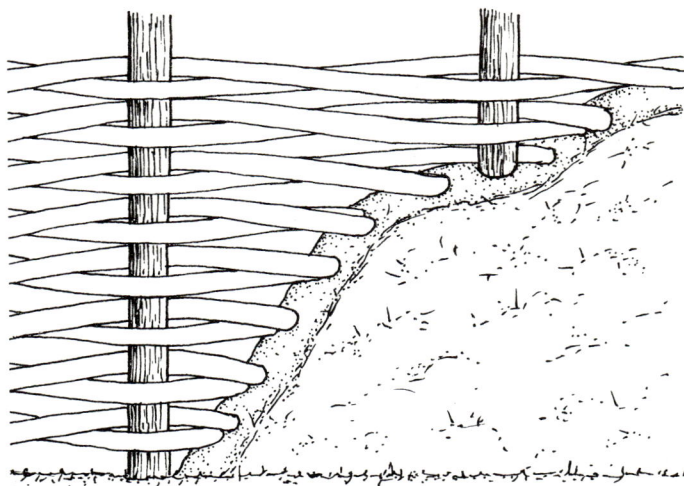

Wattle and daub was used to make the walls of some Iron Age houses. The wattles are the twigs woven between the uprights of the walls. Daub is the mixture of mud, dung, straw and animal hair that was smeared over the wattles on both the inside and outside of the walls to make them weatherproof

17

Around the houses were shallow drainage ditches to catch the rainwater from the steep thatched roofs and to prevent it from seeping under the walls into the huts; the ditches had much the same function as our gutters and drainpipes today. Piled up turves were used for the walls of one house and its roof may also have been of turf.

The people cooked, ate and slept in these houses and a family of 10 to 12 people would have lived comfortably in two such houses. Other buildings in the enclosure were used for storage. These have been identified by groups of four post-holes. They were wooden structures probably with raised floors to keep the grain or hay dry and away from rats. This must have been important at Hardwick where the land is low lying and liable to flooding. They therefore could not use storage pits which have been found elsewhere, but not at Hardwick.

A possible reconstruction of one of the four-post storage buildings found on Iron Age sites

The farm enclosure had one main entrance. A gravelled road with drainage ditches on either side led into it. The road and ditches continued for some distance away from the farm and one of the road ditches formed a boundary to the fields next to the farmstead. These were possibly cattle pastures, as the dampness of the land makes the region good for grazing but less suitable for ploughing and sowing crops. Cattle bones were found during the excavation but there was little sign of crop growing.

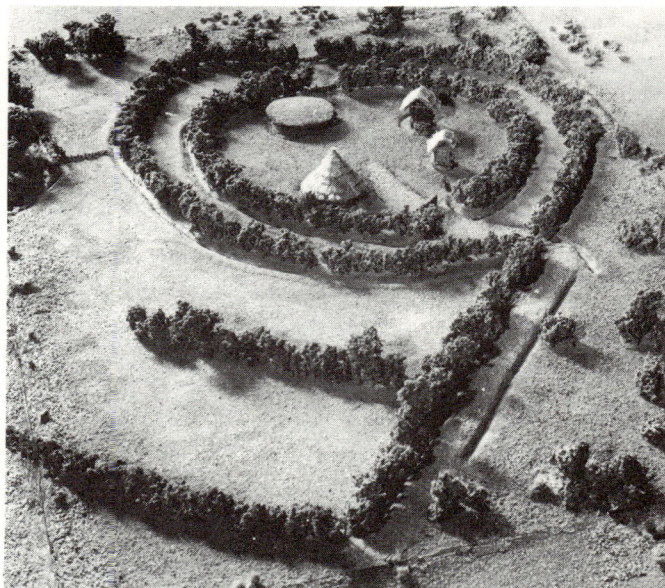

Until the site was excavated at Hardwick we had no idea of its date, of the kinds of buildings to be found there, or of the way of life of the people. Excavation has provided this evidence and enables us to build a model to show what the farm may have looked like in about 300 BC

Mousa, Shetland

Each area of Britain had its own distinctive type of Iron Age building. In the north and west of Scotland where good building stone was readily available, it was often used for houses and for fortifications. Some of the farms have tall round towers called *brochs*. These were probably built to withstand attack by people rather than wild animals. On the island of Mousa in the Shetland Islands, the broch still stands about nine metres high. It has double thickness walls with a gap of about 90 cms between, in which there are stone staircases and galleries. The outer walls are built solid with no openings except a single doorway at ground level. The tower was probably roofed as there are traces of a fireplace in the central space. There are Iron Age fields adjoining the broch although the soil seems unsuitable for growing crops. The shore and the sea must have provided a good source of food — shellfish, birds' eggs, fish and seals. Sheep and goats could have been kept on the island since they are hardy animals and require less shelter than cattle.

The Broch of Mousa

Crops and Cultivation

Large numbers of prehistoric fields have survived, and many of them, like those at Farley Mount, are of Iron Age date. They are more easily seen on the chalk downlands of Dorset and Wiltshire, on Dartmoor and in parts of Yorkshire. This land has not been extensively ploughed since the Iron Age as the soil is poor and the land hilly, so modern farming has not destroyed them. A much greater area of England where soils are richer and the land flatter must also have been ploughed in prehistoric times, but all traces of these early fields have been removed by continuous cultivation since then.

The surviving fields are small, possibly so that each one could be ploughed in a single day by two oxen pulling a simple wooden *crook ard*. This plough was

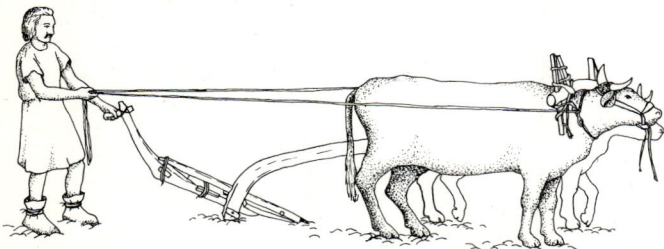

This simple wooden plough was made using archaeological evidence of pieces from Iron Age ploughs found preserved in Scotland and Denmark

sometimes tipped with an iron share. Since it only scratched a groove in the soil it was necessary to plough the fields in two directions to break up the ground thoroughly. The criss-cross patterns of prehistoric ploughing have been found cut into the chalk in several places.

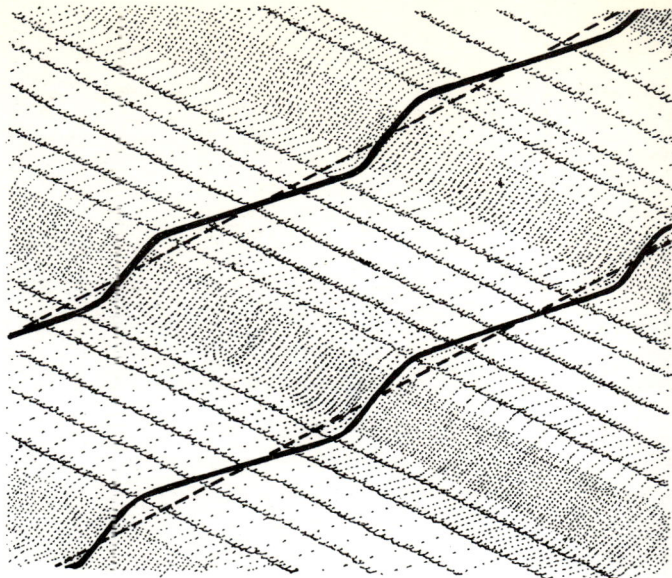

unploughed slope

ploughing begins

edges of field marked out

lynchet

If you ploughed a square plot of land on a sloping hillside, the loosened soil would gradually creep down the slope and pile up at the bottom leaving a hollow at the top. The build-up of soil is called a positive lynchet. These lynchets, which formed when the hillslopes were ploughed in the Iron Age and Roman periods, still survive in some areas today, for example at Smacen Down in Dorset. They are really a fossilization of a 2000-year-old landscape

The boundaries of fields on sloping ground are marked by *lynchets*. These are banks formed on the downhill edges of the field by the ploughed soil gradually moving downhill either by gravity or rainwash, so causing a terracing of the hill slope. Where prehistoric fields occurred on flat or more gently sloping land there were other kinds of boundaries, including small banks which may be the remains of stone walls or simply the piles of large stones cleared from the field and placed around the edge before ploughing. Fences may have been built and hedges probably grew up, but remains of these are hard to find. What do you suppose the archaeologist might look for?

The Iron Age farmers grew grain in their fields. On many excavated sites quantities of *carbonized* grain have been collected. Carbonized means that the grain has been heated enough to turn it into carbon without actually bursting into flames — like charring a piece of toast without it catching fire.

The grain was harvested by cutting the ears of corn with an iron reaping hook. If ripe and dry it was then threshed, but if damp or unripe it would have to be dried first, perhaps by placing the grain on flat stones near a fire. This may be why archaeologists find so much charred grain — some of it was likely to be overheated and become carbonized. When threshed, the grain was stored either in wooden granaries raised above the ground, as at Hardwick, or in pits which were sealed to prevent rotting and growth.

Much of the grain identified is spelt wheat and hulled barley. These are primitive types still cultivated in some parts of the world. Both these grain types were introduced into Britain at the beginning of the Iron Age. They began to replace the native wheat and barley and had the advantage that they could be sown in autumn and so ripen earlier than the spring sown varieties. This was helpful to the Iron Age farmer as his work was spread more evenly throughout the year. Rye was also grown but in smaller quantities.

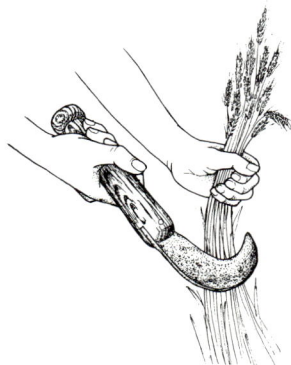

In Iron Age times corn was cut just below the ear with an iron reaping hook. The grain was then threshed and dried before being ground into flour or stored in pits. What kind of evidence do you think tells the archaeologist that corn was cut in this way?

Environmental Evidence

Plant and insect remains usually rot away but in certain circumstances they may be preserved. Cereal grains may be over-heated and turned into charcoal. The grain then retains its shape and can be identified by comparing it with present day samples of wheat and barley. To collect the carbonized grain, samples of soil are taken from pits, ditches or the floors of huts during an excavation. The earth is then mixed with water and strained through a fine-meshed sieve. The process is repeated until the light colour of the soil and water mixture shows that all the carbonized remains have been removed. The carbonized material taken from the sieve can then be identified in the laboratory.

Often extremely dry or wet conditions may preserve plants. The fungi and bacteria which cause plant material to rot cannot live without water so in very dry climates, such as in the deserts of Egypt, plants and wood may survive. In waterlogged conditions there is no air, and bacteria, fungi and animals that destroy plants and animal remains cannot exist. Under such conditions plant remains may be preserved for thousands of years. Occasionally, if the ground in which the plant or animal remains are buried is permanently frozen, specimens may also be preserved.

Plant pollen is particularly resistant to decay and may survive when all other parts of the plant have disappeared, but this too is better preserved in extremely wet or dry or frozen conditions.

In Britain only waterlogged material is available — found in peat bogs, river beds, and sometimes in the bottoms of ditches and pits if the land is low-lying. At the Iron Age farmstead at Hardwick peat samples were recovered from the bottoms of the ditches. When examined under a microscope in the laboratory, the peat was found to contain the remains of field maple trees, the seeds of guelder rose, hazel, blackthorn, elder and hawthorn. Few seeds of grassland plants survived, but the remains of beetles which live in grass and also of dung beetles showed that pasture as well as bushy scrubland surrounded the farmstead in the Iron Age.

Water flotation The soil and water are mixed and then sieved to remove the carbonized material. The heavy stones will stay in the dustbin and the light plant material is caught in the sieve

Animals

A farmer cannot plant crops in the same fields year after year without fertilizing them. The Iron Age farmer would have turned his animals out to graze on the stalks of wheat and barley which were left standing in the fields throughout the autumn and winter — except in those fields which were winter sown. In this way the fields were manured.

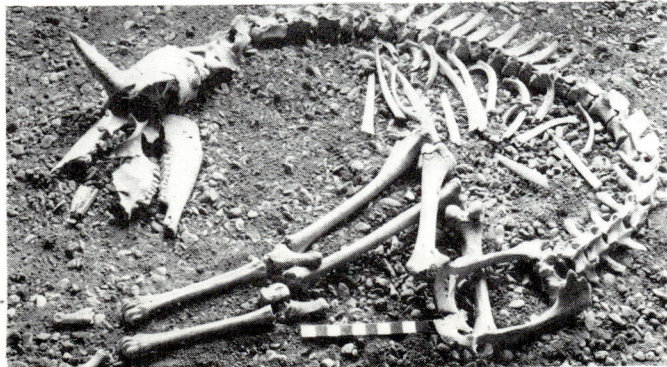

This sheep skeleton, found on an Iron Age site in Oxfordshire, is almost identical to that of a present-day Soay sheep

Cattle and sheep were the most common farm animals but some pigs were kept. We know this from the bones found on excavations. They are identified and studied and much can be learnt about the sizes of the animals, the ages at which they were killed and how they were killed. By comparing the Iron Age bones with the bones of breeds living today we can see what the cows, sheep and pigs must have looked like. The cows were quite small, similar to a modern Dexter but with longer legs. Sheep were very like the present-day Soay breed. This scraggy little sheep, which looks rather like a goat, has a coarse woollen coat that moults every spring so it does not need to be shorn like modern breeds.

The bones of horses are also found. These are similar in size and shape to the bones of the Exmoor pony. In Iron Age Britain ponies were used for pulling carts and chariots. The remains of harness and of chariots have been found but there is no evidence to show horses were ridden. Various shapes and sizes of dog skeletons are known — dogs were kept as pets and to assist with hunting and herding. Indeed Britain was famous for its hunting dogs and Strabo says they were exported throughout the Roman Empire.

23

Cooking and Pottery

The Iron Age farms produced practically all the food which the family needed. Wheat was ground into flour using quernstones and the flour was made into bread. A piece of carbonized bread was found in the excavation of an Iron Age farm near Abingdon in Oxfordshire, and the remains of clay bread ovens have been found inside houses. A kind of porridge or gruel was made from barley, and the evidence for this comes from preserved Iron Age bodies thrown into peat bogs in Denmark. The contents of the stomach of one of these people was examined and found to contain a gruel made from barley and many wild plant seeds, although we do not know if this was their daily diet.

The Roman writer Pliny tells us that grain was also made into beer, and when steeping corn to make beer, the Britons collected 'the foam that forms on the surface in the process for leaven, in consequence of which these races have a lighter kind of bread than ours'.

Animal bones have been found with knife marks from butchering, showing that a variety of meat was eaten. Beef was the main form of meat as sheep seem to have been kept largely for wool and milk. Pork was sometimes eaten as was the meat of wild animals, such as deer, hare, wild fowl and fish.

The only food which most Iron Age farmers could not produce for themselves was salt. This would have been required not only as an essential part of the diet

Wheat and barley were ground into flour using quernstones. In the early Iron Age the grain was placed on a large flat stone then rubbed with a smaller stone. Later the rotary quern was developed. The upper stone was rotated on the lower stone by means of a wooden handle while the grain was poured through the central hole in the upper stone. Try grinding your own flour with different types of stone, but do not forget to dry the grain first

Remains of simple clay ovens are found in Iron Age houses. This type is easily made using wet clay to form the dome. When the clay has dried, light a fire of twigs inside and keep it burning until the oven is thoroughly heated. Quickly rake out the ashes, place some bread dough inside and block up the doorway. When the oven has cooled break open the door and your bread will be ready

but to preserve meat stored during the winter. Remains of salt working sites have been found around the south and east coasts of Britain. The salt was extracted by allowing sea water to flow into evaporating pans either to crystallize naturally in the sun or with the help of fires. It was then packed into coarse clay containers. Large quantities of the broken containers were found at the Iron Age salt workings on the Isle of Purbeck in Dorset and fragments have been found on many inland sites showing that there was a trade in salt from the coast to the farms.

Food was cooked on an open hearth fire inside the house. The pots used for cooking were hand-made from local clay, and in the early Iron Age were simple shapes, probably made on the farms where they were used. From the third century BC a greater variety of styles with decorated and polished surfaces began to appear. Many of these were probably made by specialist craftsmen, although coarse pots of local clays continued to be made and used on the farms throughout the period. These pots were probably fired in a bonfire or pit clamp but the remains are difficult to identify.

Iron Age pottery was made very simply. When the pots had been shaped and dried, they would have been stacked in a slight hollow in the ground on straw, covered with kindling wood, and then encased in a dome of turf with sufficient holes left to let in the air so that the wood could burn. Once the fire had been lit the clamp would be left for a day or so and then taken apart. If the firing had been successful the pots would have been baked to a

hard, black finish, but occasionally the air got in and turned parts of them to a red colour. It is quite easy to fire pots in the Iron Age manner today. In the experiment shown here, the ground beneath the clamp was barely scorched and some of the straw was unburnt when all the debris was cleared away. This is probably why archaeologists have not found Iron Age pottery-making sites

Spinning and Weaving

Iron Age farmers made their own clothes of material spun and woven from the wool of their sheep. Spindle whorls — the round clay or stone weights used to make the spindle rotate evenly — are often found. So are the much larger oblong loom weights of clay and stone which were used for weighting the warp, or lengthwise, threads on an upright loom.

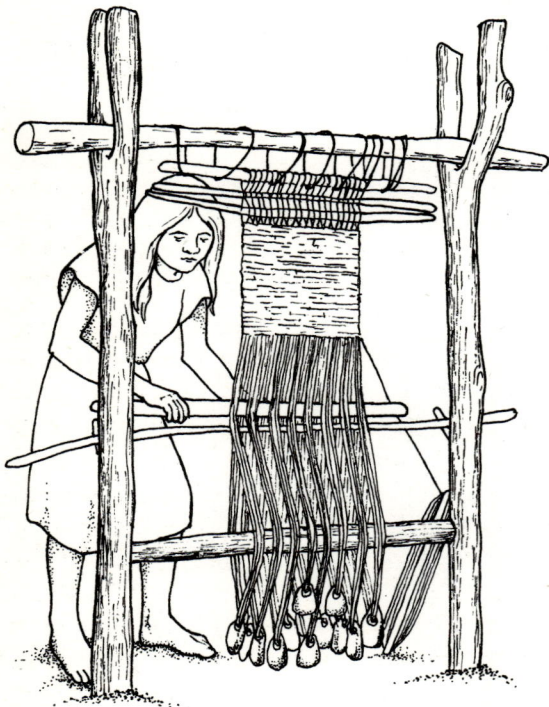

A copy of an Iron Age spindle with a clay spindle whorl

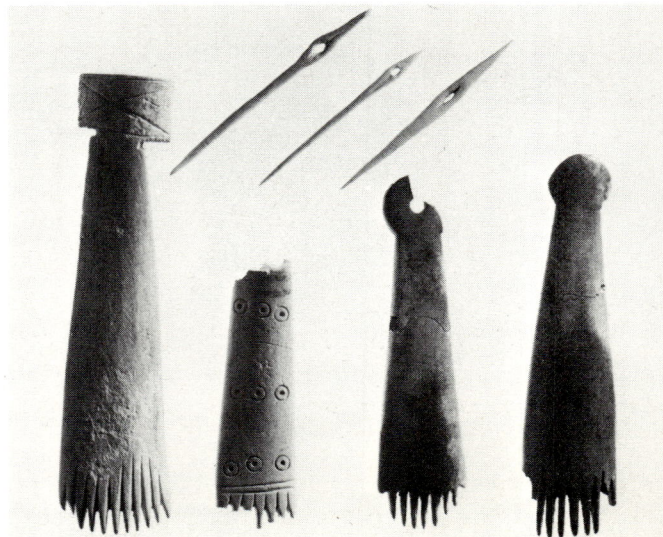

Upright weaving looms similar to this were probably used in the Iron Age but all that usually survives are oblong stone or clay loomweights for holding down the warp threads

Carved bone combs like these from Danebury hillfort were used either for plucking wool from sheep or perhaps for compacting the weft thread when weaving. The bone needles could have been for leather work or for sewing cloth

Trade

All food production, except salt, and all crafts mentioned so far show the self sufficiency of the farmsteads of Iron Age Britain, but the farms were not isolated. Nearly all excavated farmsteads produce fragments of bronze and iron, and the use of metal tools and the presence of metal jewellery show that trade was established, at least on a local basis. Iron deposits are quite common in Britain, but not every farmer would have known how to extract the ore and work it into tools. Very few furnaces have been found but slag, which is the rubbish left after iron has been smelted, is fairly widespread, showing that this was a common local industry. The local smiths made tools such as axes, adzes, saws, reaping hooks and knives.

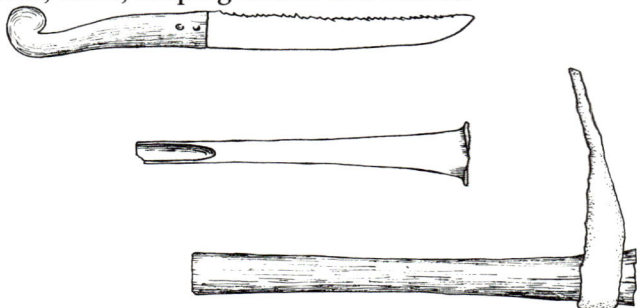

Occasionally iron tools are found in Iron Age excavations. A fine collection of woodworking tools, some with their wooden handles intact, was found buried in peat at Glastonbury

Bronze was used for making containers, brooches, rings and bracelets, and for harness fittings. Bronze smiths seem to have been travelling craftsmen and archaeological traces of bronze working are rare, although recently on a farm site in Dorset the working area of a resident bronze smith has been discovered.

Although iron was used for tools and weapons, bronze was still used for ornaments and containers. This great cauldron from Llyn Fawr in Wales, which dates to the very beginning of the Iron Age, was made from thin sheets of bronze riveted together. It would have hung over a chieftain's fire on a chain from the roof of his hut

The iron and bronze objects described above are either basic tools or simple trinkets, but from the second century BC a wider range of luxury products occur. These suggest the development of a wealthy class who could afford to have fine iron swords and daggers, and bronze shields made for show (like the ones from the River Thames). The use of gold and electrum (gold mixed with silver) for jewellery became more widespread. The heavy torques or necklets found mainly in south-eastern Britain all have a similar style suggesting that they may have come from the workshop of a master craftsman. He must have been patronized by wealthy customers, perhaps the powerful tribal chieftains who were emerging in that part of Britain.

27

Religious Behaviour

Our knowledge of religious behaviour and beliefs comes from archaeological remains which include burials, buildings and ritual deposits and from written references from the first century BC onwards which are mostly about the Druids.

In the early Iron Age the dead were usually cremated. The ashes were sometimes placed in urns and were buried in cemeteries. By the fifth century BC it seems that instead of cremation, whole corpses were buried in the cemeteries and sometimes a barrow or mound of earth was piled over the grave. In some of these burials personal possessions and even food were placed with the body — perhaps for use in the after life. In the north of Britain individuals have been found buried with a chariot and fully harnessed horses. Warriors were often buried with their swords, spears and shields as well as their brooches and other ornaments.

One of the best known female graves was discovered at Birdlip (see p. 9). Three graves encased in stones were found: the centre one contained a woman, the two on either side contained men. On the face of the woman a large bronze bowl had been placed and a smaller bowl lay near by. Other grave goods included a gilded silver brooch, rings, a bronze armlet, a knife, a necklace of amber, jet and marble and an engraved bronze mirror. The kinds of objects found must have belonged to the wealthier and more important people.

Careful burial of this sort, however, was not very common in south-east Britain. In fact many of the dead seem to have been disposed of with little ceremony. Whole bodies were thrown into rubbish pits and bits of bodies are often found. This could be because it is quite common among primitive people to expose their dead, rather than bury them. Human skulls occur in quantity at some Iron Age sites. Thirty-two fragments of human skull were found at All Cannings Cross in Wiltshire, four of which had been deliberately cut out, one had a hole in it, the others were polished by use. Perhaps these bits of skull were kept as some sort of good luck charm.

The remains of an Iron Age warrior buried with his chariot at Garton Slack, Yorkshire

Remains of ritual buildings have also been found. The best example known at present was excavated at Heathrow in Middlesex. Trenches in which wooden uprights had been placed to form the walls showed a central room. This was surrounded by a corridor or veranda made of close-set posts — only the holes for the posts remained. The building was about 10 metres square. It has been recognized as a temple because it closely resembles the later temples built by native people in the Roman period.

As well as buildings Iron Age people probably regarded certain places — rivers and marshy land for example — as sacred. The great number of fine objects thrown into the River Thames and other rivers may have a religious meaning, as may the large collection of metal work deposited in the lake at Llyn Cerrig-Bach in Anglesey.

Written evidence tells us about the Druids, who must have been a very important and powerful group of people, for Caesar says that they were responsible for the religious life of the people and acted as judges in nearly all disputes between tribes or individuals. Belief in life after death was part of their teaching and the rich objects found in graves show this. Many Druidic ceremonies were carried out in caves or woods — Pliny the Elder (first century AD) gives this description of their behaviour:

They choose groves of oak for the sake of the tree alone and they never perform any sacred rite unless they have a branch of it. They think that everything that grows on it has been sent from heaven by the god himself. Mistletoe, however, is very rarely found on the oak and, when it is, it is gathered with a great deal of ceremony, if possible on the sixth day of the moon. . . . They call the mistletoe by the name that means all-healing.

Roman writers also tell of a less pleasant ceremony of the Druids — their custom of sacrificing both animals and humans.

The Druids acted as the link between men and their gods. It seems there were many gods, who had different names in different places. Only after the Roman conquest in AD 43 are some of these names known as they were often combined with the Roman gods. For example the native stag-god Cernunnos was often associated with the Roman god Jupiter or sometimes with Mars or Mercury. Goddesses also appear, particularly the three mother goddesses — showing the traditional belief in the power of three.

Throughout the Iron Age in Britain it seems that religion and superstition played an important part in the lives of people, but we can only really begin to learn something of their beliefs and rituals towards the end of the period when written evidence is available.

The Hillforts

In this aerial view of Danebury notice how the hillfort overlooks the surrounding countryside. The excavated areas in the centre show white because the bedrock uncovered by the archaeologists was chalk

In the early Iron Age when the population seems to have been growing, large defensive hilltop earthworks were built in some parts of Britain, particularly the south. We have suggested that it must have taken many people a long time and a lot of effort to build one of these hillforts. Why, then, were they built?

One idea is that they were strongholds of the aristocracy — the chieftains and their families — who controlled or ruled over the people in the local farms. The farmers would have provided the labour for building the forts and paid dues to their lord or chief in the form of produce from the land. In return, perhaps, they would be protected in times of unrest. Another theory is that they were places where all the people of the tribe could gather for protection in troubled times, and that although there must have been a chieftain to organize construction of the fort he possibly lived elsewhere.

A further idea is that the hillforts may have begun as centres for religion like the *henges* of the Neolithic period (for example, Stonehenge which continued to be used as a temple in the Bronze Age). Yet again they could have been centres for trade — market places where people from the surrounding districts gathered at regular intervals to exchange goods, news and ideas, possibly to arrange marriages and settle other social matters. Perhaps they served as central places for both religion and trade.

Only by excavation can we begin to try and understand the real functions of Iron Age hillforts. Few hillforts have been explored on a large scale — Danebury Hill in Hampshire has added much to our knowledge of the Iron Age in this part of Britain.

Danebury

This section was cut by archaeologists through the rampart and ditch of Danebury hillfort. The person is kneeling on the original ground level which existed before the first rampart was piled up. Imagine how long it must have taken the Iron Age people to dig this ditch and pile up the rampart around the whole fort. What kinds of tools would they have used?

The defences Archaeologists cut a section through the ramparts and ditches of the Danebury hillfort to examine how and when they were built. The earliest bank and ditch encircling the hill top was probably constructed in the fifth century BC, for pottery immediately above the earliest rampart was recognized as belonging to this period. The rampart was built of chalk and soil piled up against two lines of vertical timbers. These formed a box frame which was filled with the chalk, and in front of this rampart was a ditch.

There were two entrances when the fort was first built. Some time in the third century BC the defences were greatly strengthened. The old timber fronting to the rampart disappeared and the rampart face was cut back to a steep slope continuous with the side of the ditch. The ditch was redug to a deep V-shape, and a wall of flints was built along the top of the rampart. The V-shaped ditch was cleared out regularly and the silt was thrown out on the down-hill side so that gradually an outer bank developed.

The gateways are the weak links in the defence and so at some stage during the Iron Age the west gateway was blocked. The main (east) gate has been excavated and the archaeologists discovered that it had been rebuilt ten times while the fort was in use, each time making the gate stronger than before. The first entrance in the fifth century BC was simply a gap in the rampart and ditch, with two posts on the inner side of the rampart on which gates would have been hung. This was replaced by a wider double gate which was itself rebuilt several times.

Finally at the beginning of the first century BC a major reconstruction took place in which the entrance passage was greatly lengthened to create a strongly defended corridor 50 metres long. In front of this, more earthworks were built with an outer gate.

On the flat-topped earthwork midway between the inner and outer gates a platform was created so that men armed with slings could defend the entrance. A large number of slingstones were found on this platform. From here both gates could be controlled and the whole of the entrance area and its earthworks were in view and within slingshot.

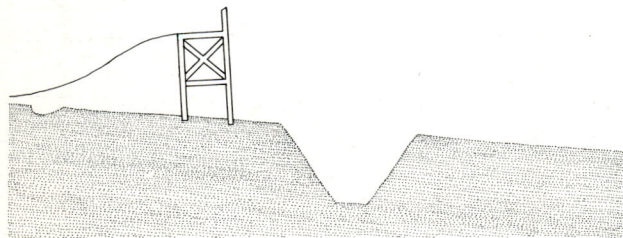

This section drawing shows how the first rampart and ditch were built at Danebury

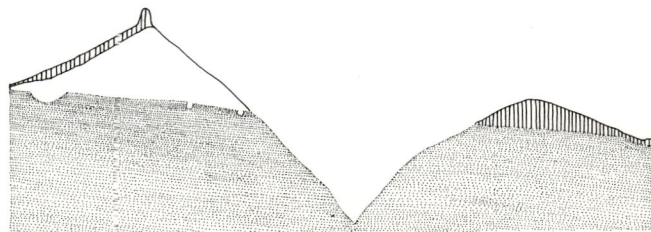

In the third century BC the rampart and the ditch were changed to look like this. Which do you think would be the more difficult of these two for the enemy to attack?

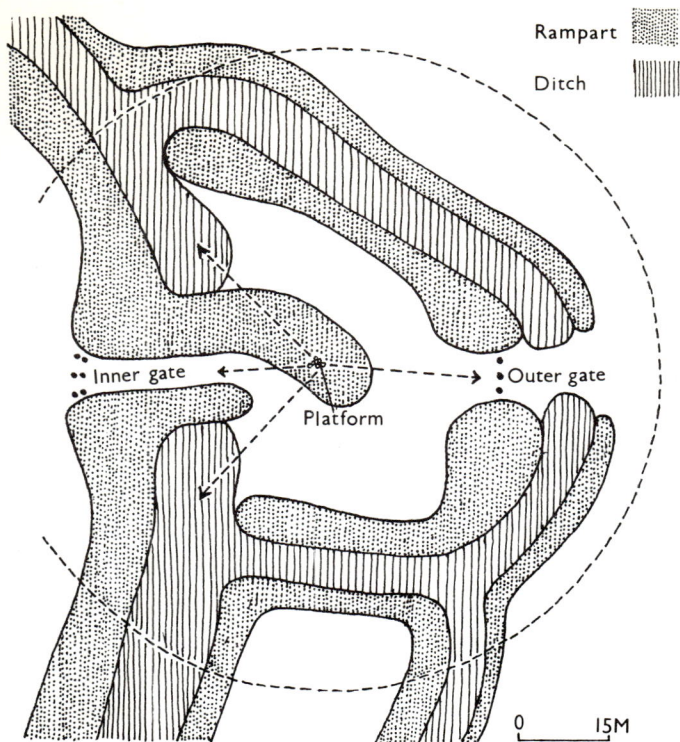

Rampart

Ditch

A plan of the east entrance of Danebury hillfort showing where the defenders stood with their slings. The circle which is indicated by a dotted line has a radius of 60 metres — the distance at which a man could be killed by a slingstone. Both gates are in range

Inner gate

Outer gate

Platform

0   15M

The excavated east gateway into Danebury hillfort. Notice the gravelled roadway leading into the fort. The lumps of flint were built up to form walls on either side of the entrance to prevent the earth sliding down onto the road

Soon after 100 BC the gateposts were burnt, the ditch was allowed to silt up and Danebury was abandoned as a permanent settlement. We do not know whether the gates were burnt deliberately and the fort deserted because it was attacked, but certainly towards the end of the Iron Age warfare had increased in south-east Britain. This is proved by the reinforcement of the defences at the eastern entrance in the later stages.

Probably the hill continued to be used occasionally — the road through the entrance passage was resurfaced in the middle of the first century AD, the rampart on the south side was heightened and the ditch partially recut. Possibly the native population were defending themselves against the Roman threat following the invasion of AD 43 although there is no evidence of a Roman attack at Danebury.

Houses and storage Inside the hillfort people lived in round houses. The houses which have been discovered so far are placed around the edges of the fort in the sheltered hollows behind the rampart. Here the fragile remains have been protected by soil washing down into the hollows from the ramparts and from the centre of the fort. There may have been many more houses in the middle, but traces of the walls and floors have been worn away by weather and later activities on the site such as tree planting.

The houses were six or seven metres in diameter and the walls were mostly of wattle daubed with a mixture of clay and dung. Lumps of the daub have been found with impressions of the wattle twigs. In some huts stakeholes which held the upright wattles of the walls have been traced. There were two post-holes for a doorway and some houses had two more posts in front supporting a porch. In at least one house the walls were made of vertical planks instead of wattles. Several of them contained the remains of hearths and clay ovens, while others had their own storage pits dug beneath the floor.

The floor of this circular house was excavated inside Danebury hillfort near the rampart. What marks the line of the walls of this house and how did the archaeologists know where the doorway was?

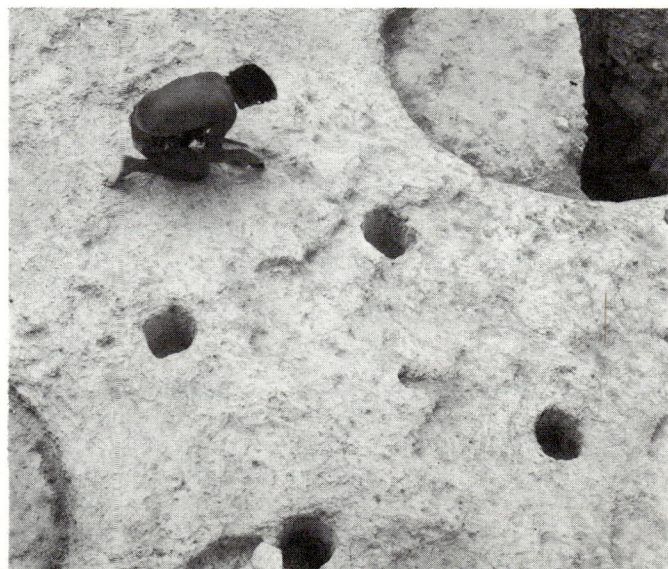

These four post-holes arranged in a square are all that remains of a small wooden building. Many groups of four postholes were found at Danebury. Compare the size of the person kneeling to the area of the building. Do you think it could have been used as a house? If not, what other possible uses could it have had?

As well as houses within the hillfort there were square and rectangular storage buildings or granaries marked by four and six post-holes. You may remember the same arrangement of four post-holes was found at the Iron Age farmstead at Hardwick. The posts would have supported small wooden buildings with raised floors. These were arranged in rows across the fort.

In almost all the excavated areas there were storage pits and more than 1000 have already been examined which means that there could have been as many as 5000 pits within the fort. Most of them were probably used for storing wheat and barley. Experiments have shown that grain will remain fresh for many months stored in pits provided they are sealed and airtight. After a year or two of use, mould and fungi would have made the pits useless for grain storage so they were abandoned. New ones were then dug and the old ones were allowed to silt up. Sometimes rubbish — broken pots, animal bones, even human bodies — were thrown into them.

The vast number of pits and the granary buildings suggest that one of the purposes of the hillfort was to protect the supply of grain produced by the surrounding community. It might also have been the centre from which the grain was redistributed.

Houses and pits were present in the hillfort from the time the first defences were constructed and they continued to be built and dug throughout the Iron Age. This probably means that there were people living in the fort all the time and that their number grew through the centuries. The number of houses in the area so far excavated suggests that there would have been between 70 and 100 houses around the ramparts by the second century BC. If houses were in the centre as well the population must have been considerable.

Pits were used for storing grain in the Iron Age. The wheat or barley would first have been dried, then placed in the pits which were then sealed over. The corn would remain fresh throughout the year until the next harvest came. There were hundreds of storage pits at Danebury, for new ones were dug when the old ones became mouldy and could no longer be used

Pits and Stratigraphy

Once the topsoil was removed from the chalk at Danebury, the pits showed clearly as dark patches. They were filled with soil and lumps of chalk. This may have been done deliberately by the Iron Age people, or they may have silted up gradually over the hundreds of years since the pits went out of use. Archaeologists try to discover when a pit was dug, what it was used for, whether it was deliberately filled or how it has silted up. To help answer these questions half the fill of each pit is removed vertically. The kind of soil is noted as it is removed. Often the colour and texture of the soil changes in layers from the top to the bottom of the pit. Pot sherds, bones and stone objects found in the *stratified layers* are placed in separate trays, one for each layer. Sometimes soil samples are taken from each layer so that they can be examined in more detail for plant remains and snail shells.

When half the pit filling has been removed, the remaining half provides a section of *stratigraphy*. A drawing is made of this, so that the different layers are recorded. The remaining half of the fill is then removed layer by layer. The oldest layers are at the bottom of the pit and any object found right at the bottom may help to tell the archeologist when the pit was being used. The plant remains and snail shells can tell us about the kind of environment that surrounded the pit when it was in use or when the layers of silt were formed.

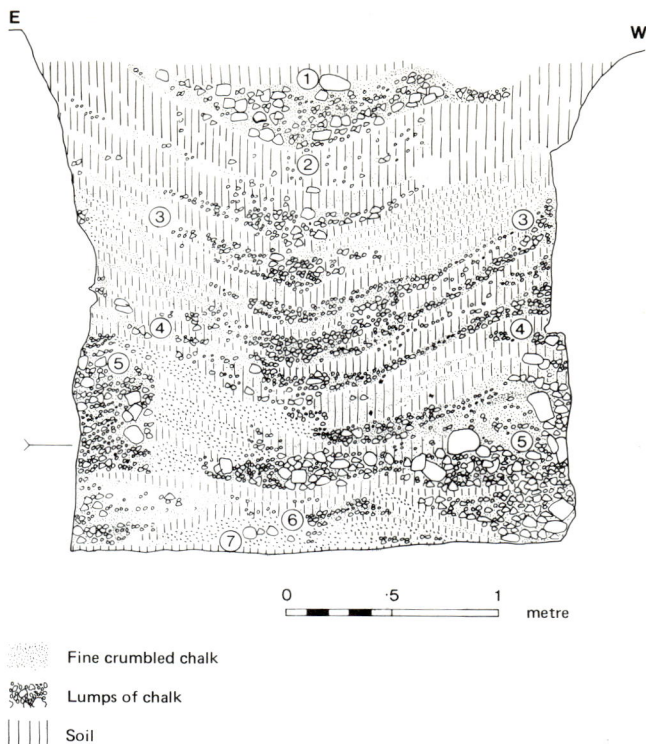

Fine crumbled chalk

Lumps of chalk

Soil

◄ In this photograph of the excavation at Danebury hillfort the pits are at various stages of being excavated. Notice the trays for the objects found in the different layers. Half the filling has been completely removed from one pit and the section is being drawn

Archaeological drawing of a pit section. The arrow shows the highest point at which tool marks were found on the sides of the pit. How do you suppose the layers of chalk and soil got into this pit?

Religion and ritual Near the centre of the fort the foundation trenches of at least four rectangular buildings have been discovered. One of the structures is very similar in plan to the Iron Age building found at Heathrow, Middlesex, which has been identified as a temple. The Danebury buildings were in use at the beginning of the first century BC but there may be earlier religious remains which have not been uncovered.

Greek and Roman writers tell us something about the religion of the Iron Age people and their ritual and superstitious behaviour. There are hints of odd ritual behaviour at Danebury. A number of horses' and cows' skulls have been found carefully placed on the bottoms of storage pits. Pots which seem to have been deliberately broken have also been found in pit bottoms. If only one broken pot or one skull had been found in a pit it might be thought to be an accident but when the same thing occurs several times we may suppose it was deliberate. Perhaps it could have been a way to please the gods.

This rectangular trench marked the foundation of an unusual building found near the centre of the fort. Such structures may have had a religious purpose. The marks of two pits lie across the corners of the rectangular trench. These pits and the building could not all have been used at the same time. Can you decide in what order they were used?

Horses' skulls were sometimes found carefully placed on the bottom of pits, often to one side

Bodies found in a pit at Danebury. Notice how carelessly they appear to have been placed in the pit

This severed human arm was found in a grave-shaped pit. There were knife marks on the bone showing that it had been cut off at the elbow

Even stranger behaviour of the Iron Age people can also be recognized at Danebury. We know from Roman writers that the Iron Age warriors cut off the heads of their defeated enemies in battle, and displayed them on the gates of their forts to show their skill as fighters. Several human skulls without bodies have been found at Danebury. Elsewhere in pits other fragments of bodies have been discovered, usually arms or legs, and some of the bones show traces of knife marks. A recent find in an early pit was the pelvis of a youth with the ends of the leg bones still in place, but chopped off just below the joints. The rest of one of the leg bones was found in the same pit — perhaps it had been split to extract the marrow for eating.

It is difficult to find an explanation for these mutilated bodies — could it be cannabalism or something to do with Iron Age surgery? What further evidence would the archaeologist need to suggest, perhaps even prove, that either of these two things were practised in the Iron Age?

Trade and exchange A large amount of pottery has been found in the fort, including simple locally made pots of the fifth and fourth centuries BC, as well as more varied pots of the third and second centuries BC, some of which were imported from quite far away in the west country. Pots were also made in the fort, for some pits containing clay have been found as well as wasters — pots that are cracked and distorted during firing.

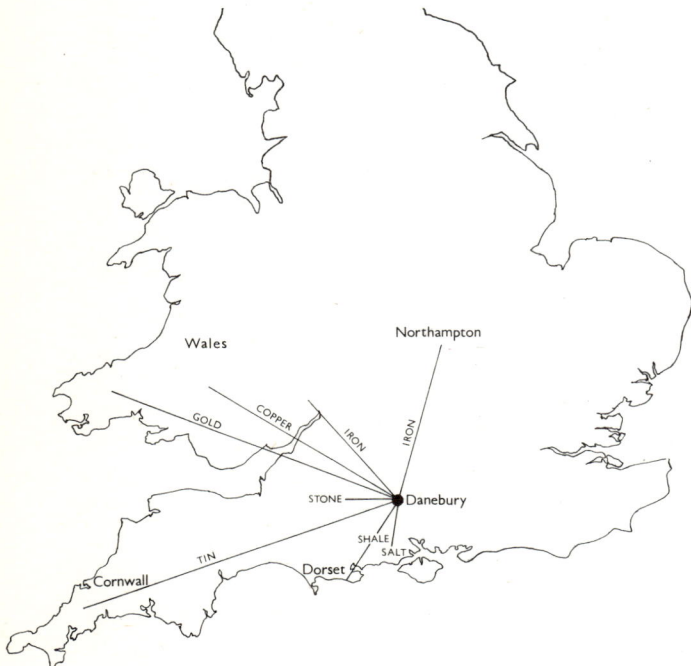

Materials brought to Danebury hillfort from all over south-west England and South Wales

Salt was brought into the hillfort from the coast — a distance of 30 miles. Many broken salt containers have been found at Danebury and it is possible that the fort served as a centre for local salt distribution. What goods might people have exchanged for the salt? Can you remember what they needed the salt for?

Shale (fragile rock) from the coast near Kimmeridge in Dorset was used for making bracelets and other jewellery in the Iron Age and finds of both unworked shale and finished bracelets at Danebury suggest that there were resident craftsmen. Bronze objects and crucibles for melting the tin and copper show that bronzesmiths too probably worked at Danebury. The tin would have been brought from Cornwall and the copper from Wales.

Iron seems to have been used a great deal at Danebury by the third century BC. Many tools have been recovered and deposits of slag suggest that raw iron was made into tools on the site. By the late second century BC raw iron was traded in the form of currency bars which look something like swords. Twenty-one

Twenty-one raw iron currency bars were found buried in a small pit at Danebury. These were a convenient shape that could easily be forged into tools or weapons if no longer needed for trading

currency bars were discovered buried in a shallow pit near the rampart. Since they were carefully hoarded they must have been of value. These bars had an actual value for they could be forged into tools. They also probably had an agreed value, just as our money has today. One bar of iron may have been worth a cow or three sheep, so they could have been exchanged many times for a variety of goods.

Iron bars are the first known example of currency used in the Iron Age. It may be that extracting iron had become a specialist skill in south-east Britain. The iron bars may have been traded to neighbouring communities which had little iron and which either hoarded the bars as wealth or made them into tools.

As well as these crafts using imported raw materials, we know from the bone combs, spindle whorls and loom weights found on the site that the usual household crafts of spinning and weaving also existed. A number of carpentry tools were found which would have been necessary for building the houses. What other things do you think the Iron Age people might have made with these wood-working tools? Both wool and timber would have been readily available from the farms close to the hillfort. We know from the environmental evidence of seeds and pollen that the countryside was more heavily wooded than today, and there are many sheep bones from Iron Age farm excavations.

The Hillfort as a Centre

What therefore was the relationship between the hill-fort and the farms around? The excavations show that Danebury was a permanent settlement for 400 years.

There were enormous facilities for storing basic food supplies, perhaps for the whole area rather than just for the people living in the fort. By the second century BC the hill top was very strongly defended and there was an additional earthwork around the fort which provided an enclosure for animals. The temple-like building and the strange examples of ritual behaviour suggest it might have been a religious centre, and the presence of much imported material, particularly salt, iron and shale, supports the idea of the fort as a centre of trade.

DANEBURY

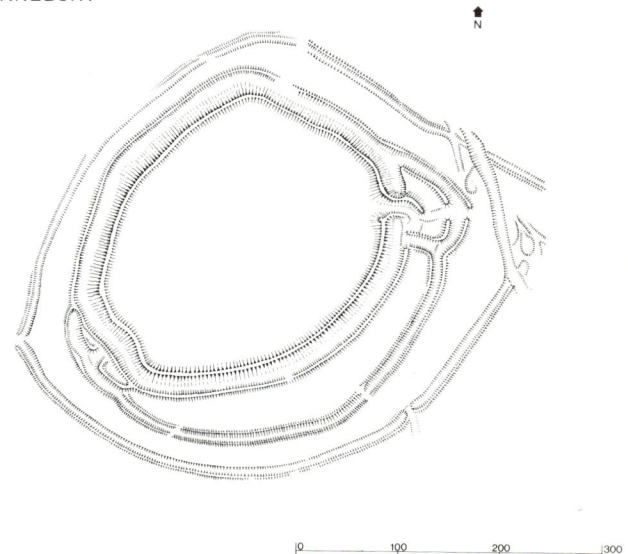

The hillfort of Danebury consisted of three separate enclosures. The inner one in which people lived was strongly protected. What could the outer enclosures have been used for?

No evidence of a chieftain living in the fort has been found but large defended farm sites such as Little Woodbury in Wiltshire are well known. The house there was large and seems grand enough to have been the home of an important person. Perhaps the hillforts then were communal places belonging to the tribe as a whole, some of whom lived there while others, including the chieftain, lived in the farms around. The whole tribe, however, will have used the fort for trading purposes, to worship the gods, to store surplus grain and as a safe retreat when an enemy attack was threatened. In other words the hillfort was the centre of the territory belonging to the tribe.

It is possible that later in the period the people of the hillfort concentrated on raising animals and that the surrounding farms produced the grain. The many indications of specialized crafts and industries in the hillfort from the second century BC onwards might further suggest that many of the inhabitants were not involved in farming at all, but were full-time manufacturers supplying goods for the territory for which the hillfort was the centre. Could the development of hillforts like Danebury have marked the beginnings of towns in Britain?

Contact with the Roman World

After 100 BC the people of Britain had increased contacts with the people of the continent. This is shown by imported foreign goods such as brooches, metal containers and coins found in the south-east, particularly around the river Thames. These goods came mostly from northern France and must have been brought by traders. Early in the first century BC there were also trading links between the south coast of Britain — Hampshire, Dorset, Devon and Cornwall — and the coasts of Brittany (the area then called Armorica) and Normandy. A scatter of Armorican coins has been found along the south coast.

Caesar tells us that groups of people from Belgica (northern France and Belgium) settled along the coast of Britain, most of them keeping the names of their tribes. Caesar's campaigns in Gaul must have forced the people of northern France to look to Britain for support and trade and eventually as a place to settle.

We can tell by the way of life of the people in south-east Britain that new people were moving into the area to live. The people who came were interested in trade for they came from regions which had closer contact with the Roman Empire, where trade was all important for the survival of the Roman way of life. The newcomers built large new enclosures (*oppida*) in valleys so that they controlled river crossings. They were concerned with guarding the routeways rather than with a strategic view point on a hill top. Gradually the hillforts were abandoned as far west as the Salisbury region.

The hillfort was built earlier in the Iron Age. It was probably abandoned in favour of the much later valley fort or *oppidum*. Later still the Romans realized the importance of the site near a river crossing and they built a town nearby. The site of this town is still in use today

After the invasions of Caesar in 55–54 BC the southern tribes with whom he made treaties, including the Trinovantes and the Catuvellauni, traded increasingly with the Roman world. They imported wine and oil in great quantities in large jars called *amphorae*. Pieces of amphorae are found on many late Iron Age sites. In the burial mound of a chieftain at Welwyn, Hertfordshire, amphorae were found with silver cups, bronze tableware including jugs and bowls, and a set of glass gaming pieces all imported from various parts of the Roman Empire. Most of the imports discovered by archaeologists are luxury items but Strabo tells us the Britons exported in exchange corn, cattle, gold, silver, hides and skins, slaves and hunting dogs.

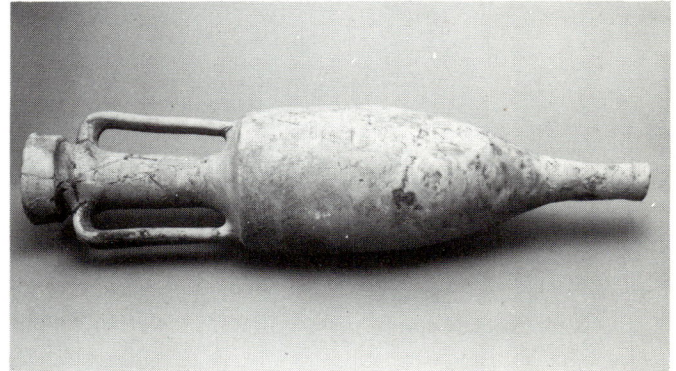

Iron Age chieftains loved luxury. As the Roman armies moved across Europe towards Britain it became gradually easier for the natives of Britain to obtain luxury goods. One thing that was imported to the island in great quantity was Italian wine. It was transported in large containers called amphorae. Fragments of amphorae are sometimes found in Iron Age settlements and complete ones, probably full of wine, were occasionally buried with dead chieftains

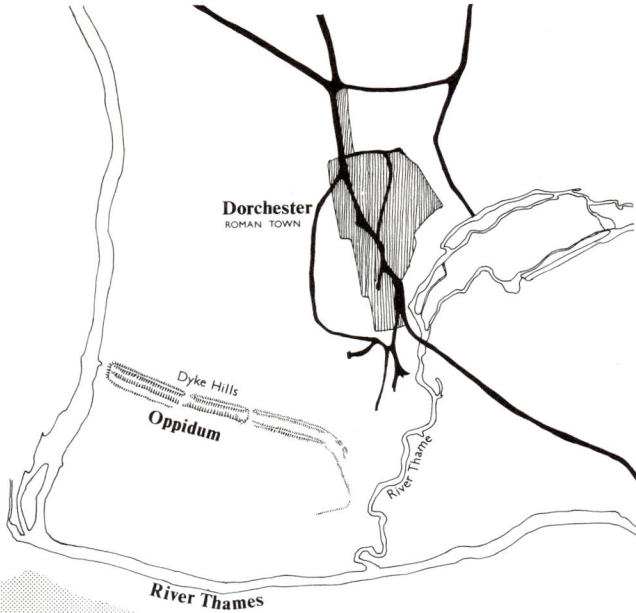

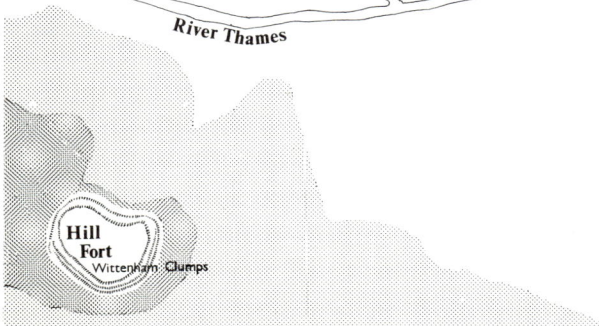

43

◄ The chieftain buried at Welwyn in Hertfordshire was well provided with wine for feasts in the life after death. He was also buried with two fine silver cups imported from Italy, a board game of which the glass gaming pieces survive and other foreign luxury goods

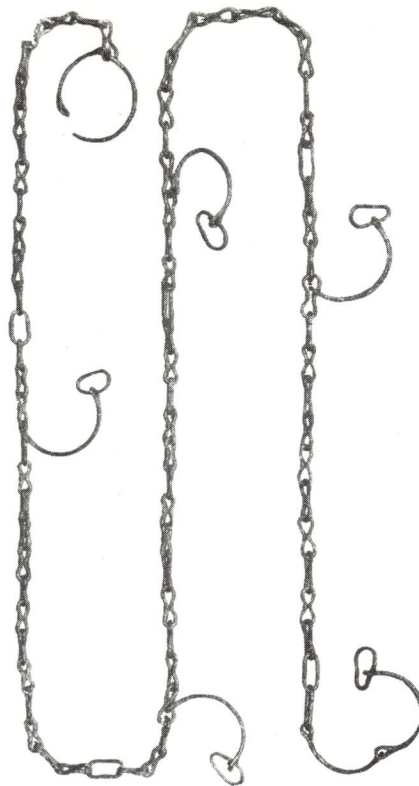

Caesar says there were two privileged classes of people, the Druids and the warriors, and that 'the common people are treated almost as slaves, never venture to act on their own initiative, and are not consulted on any subject'. Although this may be an exaggeration there certainly was a slave trade. Chains for linking slaves together by the neck have been found at Llyn Cerrig Bach, Anglesey, and in several places in south-east England. Slaves were widely used in the wealthy Roman world and slave trading in Britain probably developed rapidly following Caesar's invasions.

To pay for imported luxuries the Britons had to provide exports for the Roman market. It seems that there was a lively trade in slaves. Groups of slaves would have been chained together by the neck with great slave chains like this one found at Bigbury in Kent

Britain had long been famous for mineral wealth. Tin from Cornwall had been exported to the Mediterranean countries since at least the fifth century BC. Iron was readily available, and more and more gold and silver was extracted after 100 BC when coins began to be used instead of iron currency bars. The heavy torques made of gold often mixed with silver worn by the British chieftains must have attracted the attention and envy of the Romans. Britain's reputation for mineral wealth was one of the reasons why the Emperor Claudius invaded Britain in AD 43.

Gradually more tribes were influenced by the new ideas from the continent. The use of coinage spread and tribal chieftains minted their own coins, often bearing their names. This marks the first appearance of writing in Britain. By the beginning of the first century AD most of the tribes of central England were minting and using coins. They were also making pots that were copies of imported types and were using a potter's wheel. Some tribes, like those in Dorset, clung to old traditions. They minted coins but continued to live in hillforts until the Roman invasion of the middle of the first century AD when General Vespasian and the Second Legion attacked and took over 20 hillforts along the south coast. Only south-west England, Wales and the north had remained virtually unchanged in their way of life since the early Iron Age.

Towards the end of the Iron Age, people in south-east Britain ► minted their own coins. Coins were very useful for giving as presents, for hoarding as wealth and for buying and selling in the market. Their appearance in Britain coincides with the period when trade with the continent increased

By the time the Roman army invaded in AD 43, the people of south-east Britain had been in contact with the Roman world for 100 years and so it is not surprising that the conquest should be rapid in that area and that 11 'kings', that is tribal Chieftains, were prepared to surrender to Rome immediately. This we know from the inscription on the triumphal arch in Rome erected by the Emperor Claudius to commemorate his conquest of the barbarian tribes beyond the ocean. The promise of peace and greater chances for trade and acquiring wealth and luxuries must have been most attractive to the increasingly civilized people of this part of Britain.

Sites to Visit

Prehistoric Fields
Good examples of fields and trackways are still visible in many parts of Britain. They can be seen best early in the morning or late in the evening when the sun is low and the banks cast long shadows. Some of the better examples are —

Fyfield Down, Wiltshire (Grid ref. SU140710)
Kingston Down, Dorset (Grid ref. SY957780)
Chaldon Herring, Dorset (Grid ref. SY795805)

Experimental Prehistoric Farm
An ancient farm has been reconstructed on Butser Hill to test theories of prehistoric house building, farming methods etc. As well as the research site, there is a demonstration site open to the public which has a round house based on the plan of an excavated Iron Age house. There are fields with livestock and demonstrations are given of agricultural methods and manufacturing techniques. The demonstration site is at Queen Elizabeth Country Park, Butser Hill, Nr. Petersfield, Hants.

Hillforts
There are a large number of hillforts and those with surviving earthworks are usually marked on Ordnance Survey maps. Many are on private land and permission to visit them should be obtained from the land-owner.

Danebury Hill
— 3 miles N.W. of Stockbridge, Hants. This site belongs to Hampshire County Council and is open to visitors at all times.

Maiden Castle
— 2 miles S.W. of Dorchester, Dorset. The site belongs to the Department of the Environment and is open at all times. Finds from the excavations are on display in the Dorset County Museum, Dorchester.

South Cadbury Castle
— Somerset. This Iron Age fort has four great banks and ditches and at least two entrances. The site has been excavated and was proved to have been refortified in Saxon times. For further information read *Cadbury Camelot* by Leslie Alcock (Thames & Hudson).

Uffington Castle and White Horse
— Berkshire. A hillfort with a single rampart and ditch, broken by one entrance facing west. Nearby, the white horse is cut into the turf of the chalk downland. Its design resembles that found on certain late Iron Age coins and metalwork. It is therefore usually thought to be Iron Age in date. Department of Environment site, open at all times.

Museums
Many county and town museums possess Iron Age material from local excavations, but much of the high quality metalwork of the period is displayed in the British Museum.

Acknowledgments

Photographs
J R Boyden, p. 15
C Bradford, p. 18
Bristol United Press, p. 23 (far right)
British Museum, pp. 8, 9, 11, 13, 14, 43, 44, 44, 45
Cambridge University, p. 16
Corinium Museum, Cirencester, p. 29
Crown Copyright, pp. 4, 19, 21, 30
Danebury Trust, pp. 7, 31–40 (all photos)
Department of the Environment, p. 28
Faber and Faber Ltd, p. 8
City Museum and Art Gallery, Gloucester, pp. 9, 12
P Harrison, p. 26
Institute of Archaeology, pp. 26, 41
Manchester Museum, p. 44 (right)
Nationalmuseet, Copenhagen, p. 10
National Museum of Wales, pp. 13, 27
Oxfordshire Archaeological Unit, pp. 16, 22
Oxfordshire County Museum, p. 23 (bottom left)
Peter Reynolds, p. 23 (right)
Simon Warner, p. 23 (top left)

Line Drawings
Debby Ross